Tactical Magick
Seth

Tactical Magick

by Seth

Copyright © 2004

Lulu Enterprises, Inc.

All rights reserved by the author. No part of this publication can be reproduced, stored in a retrieval system, or transmitted in any form or by any means, electronic, mechanical, photocopying, recording or otherwise, without the prior permission of the publishers and/or authors.

While every precaution has been taken in the preparation of this book, Lulu Enterprises assumes no responsibilities for errors or omissions, or for damages resulting from the use of information contained herein. The appearance and contents of this book are the sole responsibility of the author.

Table of Contents

INTRODUCTION 5
WHAT IS TACTICAL MAGICK? 6
HERMETIC INFLUENCES 7
THE BASICS 8
MAGICAL SENSES 11
THE LOGRIS 14
SHIELDS 17
SPELL TRAJECTORY 22
HOT SPOTS 24
OCCULT MACHINES 28
OUIJA BOARDS 33
SUBVERTING REALITY 38
CRISIS ENERGY 40
OMNIMANCY 43
MAGICAL COMBAT 47
MAGICK BY ROTE 56
WORKING WITH A GROUP 60
THE TOOLBOX 65
EXPANDING WORLDVIEW 67

Magick is cheap, and power is all around you.

Introduction

The purpose of this book is to provide you with magical tech and survival skills. Techniques, technologies, and skills that will give you an edge in living with magick in the harsh and beautiful realm that is reality. Their purpose is to illustrate the use of magick to resolve situations effectively, which is the result of the incorporation of magick, requisite skills, and their usage into one's daily life. The goal is to promote understanding of the role of magick as both a tool and as a method of spiritual enrichment, though the material presented within is a magical system primarily concerned with results and situation resolution. A system that incorporates anything and everything depending upon personal relevance and usefulness. Tactical Magick is a book that presents a way of taking magick out of the inner sanctum and onto the streets of the real world. This is results magick right to the core.

What is Tactical Magick?

A banishing ritual done with a bic lighter and salt packets in a cheap hotel room. Possum skull house guardians and scarecrow golems in the cornfield. Teddy bear exorcisms and beating down the bogeyman with a watergun. Scrying for the future with a brick and pirated music. Turning a roadtrip into a vision quest with a mixed tape and a good friend. Punching your enemy right in the soul. Evoking a god with sidewalk chalk and cheap red wine in an alley. Its Molotov magick that burns away the obstacles in your life, if you have the power.

This is for the soldier who dodges a bullet, the graffiti artist who evades arrest, the beggar who walks with the spirits of the street. The college student who needs to pass the final exam, the gangbanger trying to survive another score, the starving artist who has to hold on for one more month. This is for the stock broker who has to make or break the deal, the twenty-something looking for a path in life, the police officers and firefighters who don't want to become more names on a wall. The stripper trying to raise a child by herself, the anarchist who wants to change the system, and the politician that is his enemy.

This is for you, so step up.

Hermetic Influences

Tactical magick, in many ways, is a magical system built upon the eclectic and situational use of symbols, associations, and relationships in order to create effective magical manifestations of the will. As such, it has no foundation beyond the daily lives of its practitioners. Though however incomplete, the following hermetic magical document is an effective glimpse into the fundamental elements of this approach to magick.

The Emerald Tablet

I. Truly, without deceit, certainly and absolutley-
II. That which is Below corresponds to that which is Above, and that which is Above corresponds to that which is Below, to accomplish the Miracle of One Thing.
III. And just as all things have come from One, through the Meditation of One, so all things proceed from this One Thing in the same way.
IV. The Sun is its Father. Its Mother is the Moon.
V. The Wind has carried it in his Belly. It is nourished by the Earth.
VI. It is the father of every Perfected Thing in the whole World. Its Power is complete if it is converted into Earth.
VII. Separate the Earth from the Fire, the subtle from the gross, gently and with great care.
VIII. It rises from the Earth to Heaven, and descends again to the Earth,
IX. And thereby receives Power from Above and Below
X. By this means, you shall obtain the Glory of the whole World. All Obscurity will be clear to you. This is the strong Power of all Power. It overcomes everything subtle and penetrates everything solid.
XI. In this way was the World created. From this there will be amazing Applications, of which these are the means.
XII. Therefore I am called Thrice Greatest Hermes, holding three parts of the Wisdom of the whole World.
XIII. Herein have I completely explained the Operation of the Sun.

The Basics

There are a multitude of books, tapes, workshops, and articles that focus on what are considered to be the basics of magical practice. As such, there will be no exhaustive discourse on these elements. However, there are three basic aspects of magical practice that are of great importance to the understanding and capacity to interact with the concepts presented in this text, and pursuant to this will be presented in a limited fashion here. These basic elements are physical fitness, meditation, and energy manipulation.

Despite how much we may or may not view the flesh as a prison, after a gnostic fasion, we are beings housed in and a part of the physical realm. Keeping the body, this temple, at peak condition is important to any magical endeavor. When the body is good physical condition there is an abundance of vitality, awareness, and endurance, all of which are important faculties in magical practice. This is best done through balanced diet, consistant exercise, uninterrupted restful sleep, and good personal hygene. When the body is well rested as a result of sleep, full of vitality as a result of a balanced diet, refreshed by cleanlieness, and poised from exercise, the magus is ready to engage in effective magical practice. Not only will these healthy habits improve the quality of your life, but also the potency, duration, and precision of your magick.

Meditation is a cornerstone of magical practice, though is not as rigid as one might think. There are a multitude of theories and methods of meditation, in fact, it is not the act of meditation that is of importance, it is the resulting state of relaxed readiness that is the goal. The most simple meditation technique is to find a comfortable physical position, though not one that will encourage the practitioner to fall asleep unexpectedly (hence the common usage of an upright or sitting position). Once in place, the practitioner begins to breath deeply, not hyperventilating, but drawing breath all the way down into the lower parts of the lung, and breathing out in a controlled and slow manner. Eventually the mind will sharpen and the body will relax, creating the ideal state of relaxed readiness. It is from this state of relaxed readiness that effective magick springs forth. In time the practitioner will become adept at achieving this R&R state with a single controlled breath, allowing them to prepare for empowered magical action at a moment's notice.

Energy manipulation, like fitness and meditation, is discussed at length in many texts and sources external to this book, though a brief overview will be given. Magical energy, as the fundamental element of any magical endeavor, must be manipulated by the practitioner in order to manifest the will. There are a plethora of theories and techniques regarding energy manipulation, and it is likely that the reader of this book is already well versed in such techniques, though some things bear repeating. Energy must first be sensed, this can be done with a combination of the 'magical senses' which will be discussed later in the book and the act of visualizing the energy you are being faced with in whatever manner is most compatible with your personal worldview. Once the energy is sensed you must reach out with your will and take control of that energy, shaping it into patterns of your choosing, or using the pre-existing patterns as you see fit. This is the most basic element of magick, and is heavily reliant upon the strength of your will and your belief in the existence of magick itself. Once the energy is shaped it can be used for the magical sending or spell you are attempting to produce. When the magical act has been completed, ground the leftover energy by projecting it into either an object, the earth itself, or dissipating it into the ambient environment. Naturally, the most basic spell is the energy ball. Simply draw upon the ambient magical energy, shape it using visualization and your will, then infuse it with your intent and project it towards the target. When you have mastered these basics, the world of magick is an open door.

Magical Senses

In order for a practitioner to become a dynamic force of change, that practitioner must have the ability to perceive the reality in which he or she is working. The aspiring magus must develop what can easily be called 'magical senses'. Much like sight, sound, taste, touch, and smell, these senses must be recognized and developed in order for the practitioner to be able to interact with and manifest the will within reality. These senses for the most part mirror the standard five senses, though some extend past those five and become what many people refer to as the sixth sense and beyond. This is the occult art of observation and perception.

How can a sorcerer hope to interact with spirits if they cannot be sensed? How powerful can the changes wrought in reality be if the mage who manifests those changes cannot perceive the results of the exertion of her will? If a warlock is cursed and does not have the magical senses necessary to notice, what hope has he of countering it? These are the sorts of problems that a practitioner without developed magical senses can find themselves dealing with. The development and constant maintenance of these senses is of the utmost importance, because it is these senses that will allow the adept to observe and perceive situations and deal with them as they arise. A magus at the top of his game is proactive and preemptive, not blindly reactionary.

The most effective training method is a visualized expansion of awareness that in time becomes actual magical awareness. First achieve a meditative state, either through personal meditation techniques or whatever mental or physical methods the individual uses to enter a state of calm. Once you have settled into this state, begin to expand your awareness. Try to visualize your room in your mind's eye, see without seeing. Now combine your other senses with this mental picture. Hear the room, and use the ambient sound to construct that same mental picture. Then create that picture with smell and taste. Try to create the picture with touch, this will require you to visualize your sense of touch extending far beyond your physical body. Imagine the textures of the various objects in the room, the walls, and the floor. Once you have created the picture in your mind, try to create it using all five of your senses at once. Sight will naturally come the most easily, but once you see the room try to hear it with your eyes open. Now, while watching and listening to the room, smell, taste, and touch it. The point of this exercise is to illustrate to the practitioner that even the common human senses can be used with much more detail, precision, and range when coupled with creative visualization.

After considerable practice expanding the five senses, now it is time to discover and develop the magical senses. For the most part magical senses are types of energy perception, a good metaphor would be that a magus who has developed magical senses can perceive not only other realms, external entities, but the very fabric of reality. The best way to being training in these senses is to repeat the above exercises, though instead of perceiving the physical elements of the room, use sight, hearing, taste, touch, and smell to become aware of the energy patterns that make up the physicalities of the room. It would be beneficial at this point to add a few magical items to the room, perhaps the sorcerer's ritual dagger or a ceremonial vessel. For the most part the physical objects in the room will feel magically just like they do with the standard senses. However, when perceiving magical items the mage will be able to hone the senses to an awareness of the magical properties of the items. At the most basic levels of skill the mage will be able to tell a magically charged item from a mundane item, be able to pick out the empowered dagger from an entire collection of knives for example. The more developed this sense becomes, the magus will be able to perceive what sorts of magical energies permeate the items, allowing the magus to divine elements of the item's origins and purpose.

The same techniques hold true for external entities and places of power. The more aware of energy patterns in reality the witch becomes, the better able she will be to interact with those elements of reality. For example, when a witch walks into a building she can use her magical senses to determine if it is haunted, where in the building the primary manifestations are taking place, and to some degree what sort of entity is doing the haunting. By developing an occult awareness, the practitioner will be able to discern details about reality that can be very useful. Imagine how much of an advantage you would have if one had the ability to tell practitioner from non-practitioner with a mere glance, or be able to tell when someone or something is looking for or at you. It is important to have the ability to perceive, communicate, and interact with entities, magical constructs, or complex enchantments and magical items.

In essence, every magus has the ability to develop what many call the 'second sight'. It is the ability to perceive and observe magical energy patterns. Though with the aide of visualization the magus will be able to expand these senses to a range much greater than the physical body. Some practitioners may require ritual items or physical foci to help them to maintain and focus this awareness, like enchanted monocles or perhaps a talisman of 'seeing', though these senses can be developed without such augmentations. Once the mage becomes aware of reality, then the manifestation of the magi's will is much more powerful and precise.

The Logris

The majority of this chapter is borrowed from one of the author's previous titles, Post-Modern Magick. While readers familiar with that work may feel this to be overly repetitious, readers new to the concept will require the reprinted material in order to better understand the later part of the chapter, which will deal with creating what are called spell protocols that can be stored in the Logris field.

The Logris, in a classical sense, is a dynamic symbol of Chaos, better known as the chaosphere or chaos wheel. While keeping this original meaning as a reference the word Logris can also be used to describe the staging area for spells within the "aura" of any magus, like a membrane or energy field of sorts that surrounds the magus. While much argument and essay could be held in defining and investigating the aura itself, that will not be done here. Instead, the word aura will be defined loosely as the collection of energy fields that permeate and surround the magus. One of these energy fields is the Logris. For those who are aware of its existence and skilled enough to use it, the Logris can serve as both a medium for the casting of spells and an amplifier for the power of the spell.

The theory and procedure are as follows: Much like various parasites that graft themselves to the skin or aura of humans and magi alike, just so can a spell be attached, or "hung" on the Logris energy field, almost like a temporary tattoo on the skin. The magus first casts the majority of the spell. Once the spell is complete, but not sent, the spellcaster visualizes the Logris field. When the Logris has been raised the spellcaster puts the spell onto the Logris. Perhaps visualizing physically hanging the spell on a wall, peg, or the shimmering surface of a forcefeild. By doing so practitioner will be able to effectively store up spells until they are needed. At that point there are two things that can be done. The practitioner, finding his or herself in need of quick and powerful magick, could pull one of these spells off the Logris.

This acts as a power multiplier for the spell. First there is energy put into the spell itself, added to the power used to activate the stored spell and push it out of the Logris. Then there is the additional energy boost from the spell's passage through the Logris itself. Thus making a most potent spell indeed. Effectively allowing the spells cast by that magus to have a potency much greater than the caster himself.

This technique also allows the caster to perform lengthy and complex ceremonial or formulaic magick, then store the spell to use at their leisure. Thus making the practice of ceremonial magick much more effective in situations requiring immediate action and result. However, one must always remember that the laws of thermodynamics also, at times, apply to magical energy. The amount of power and thus number of spells that can effectively hang on the Logris depends greatly upon the power and energy capacities of the magic user himself. Once a spell is hung on the Logris it begins to decay like an unused muscle or a leaking barrel of gunpowder. Depending upon how much power was put into the original spell, it will take a small portion of that to maintain the spell's potency over long periods of time. As a result most magic users who employ the Logris technique either hang several spells that they intend upon using soon, or they store only a few potent ones and then hold onto until just the right moment.

A final exciting benefit from using the Logris often is that the energy field is gradually effected by the spells hung upon it. So the observant, patient, and powerful magus could use this knowledge to cast the same spells often. Over time the Logris will begin to "remember" spells often hung upon it, and once the adept becomes the master the Logris will evolve from being merely a storehouse and amplifier, but also providing immediate access to a multitude of spells regularly cast though it. A living grimoire.

These impressions made upon the Logris that allow it to 'remember' spells that are used often are what can be referred to as 'spell protocols'. These function much like sigils, in that they can be empowered and cast a specific spell with few steps or preparation. Though instead of walking around with a pocketful of sigils (though a valid even if haphazard technique), the active magus with many protocols etched into the Logris from constant use has the entirety of these protocols on hand without the need for piles of paper or any sort of organization. Often the Logris can 'load and execute' a protocol of a specific type when the magus is casting a spell even if the magus does not consciously choose to use a protocol.

While the Logris remembers frequently cast spells, and in time they become incorporated into the field as protocols, the industrious and creative magus can actually consciously 'etch' protocols into the Logris at will. The practitioner would focus on creating the spell, painstakingly focusing on every detail of the spell's construction to that once the spell is ready to send, it is sent directly into the Logris itself, essentially 'uploading' it to the Logris field. Henceforth, the spell protocol is available to the magus when such a spell or one similar are needed, then that protocol is summoned forth, augmented where necessary to fit the situation, then sent on its way. Some might call this a subtle form of hyper-sigil magick, because this technique can be used outside the Logris as well, infusing spell protocols into occult devices or including them in the creation of magical entities.

Shields

The knowledge of shields and the mastery of their usage is a vital component in the repertoire of a modern magus. This world is full of magick, and much of it is of a kind that you may not want to be in contact with it. Besides, it is much more efficient to be prepared with shielding techniques than merely react to stimulus with protection spells or countermagick. Shields are, in essence, personal energy fields constructed for the purpose of acting as an energy filter and a defense grid when needed. This chapter will illustrate shield creation and usage as well as the practitioner's natural defenses.

The first step is to come up with a personal visualization for shields and how they work when used. Most practitioners encounter thus far by the author tend to use what can be said as the force field model. They see their shields as energy fields that harden and flex when attacked, much like fictional shields in Star Trek or Star Wars. As the threats vary, they visually alter the 'frequency' of the shields to adapt. Though other visualizations are available, the imagination of the practitioner is the only real limitation. Shields could be seen as the actual historical devices that materialize to stop the incoming threat as it nears the practitioner, or it could be a metaphysical membrane that surrounds the practitioner that blocks or absorbs the threat much like its biological counterpart, the possibilities are endless. Shields encompass a space much of the same size as a person's aura, and thus vary from person to person. They can, with increased energy expenditure, be made to cover an area much greater if the controller of the shield has the focus and skill to maintain the integrity of the field at such sizes. Normally shields are powered by the practitioner's personal power reservoirs, though depending upon the practitioner's ability and resources, may be hooked up to and empowered by external sources. These sources can be other magi, places of power, stored energy repositories, or energy drawn from the immediate environment. In most cases the amount of power fed to the shields will relate directly to their strength, though a skillful manipulation of that energy is required to adapt the shield to the particular situation or a multitude of threats with different methods of attack.

The particular visualization of a shield will greatly affect the exact methods in which the shield is powered, adapts to threats, and is used when the time comes. To illustrate we will use two examples. First, the force field style of shield. Most practitioners who employ this sort of shield usually only have it nominally powered during times of perceived safety or 'downtime'. When a situation arises, they in essence use their magical will to give the 'shields up' command, and they begin to rapidly send energy into the energy patterns of the shield. Depending upon their skill in energy manipulation, the shields will grow to their full power very quickly or gradually. As the threats vary in number and type, the practitioner visualized a change in their shield's 'frequency' or 'recalibrate' the field in order to deal with the new threat. Most practitioners using the force field style of shield use, in addition to their personal power, external sources. Most of these sources are connected with visualizations of power cables, tendrils of pure energy, or sigils that funnel power directly into the shield. The second example, the membrane style of shield, is much different. Practitioners who use this style of shield tend to keep it somewhat more charged at all times than the force field style practitioners. This gives them the advantage of being more difficult to affect when caught off-guard, though at any given time much more of their energy is directed towards maintaining their shield, and so may not be as aware of their environment or able to push greater quantities of energy into other directions without first withdrawing some from their shields. Membrane shields tend to function in a very organic manner, so have several methods of threat elimination. One way is for the membrane to harden, like chitin or tough skin, in order to simply deflect the incoming threat. Though the second method is the most versatile, even as it is the more difficult. The shield can be made to work like an external immune system in that it engulfs and dissipates (digests) the incoming threat. This has several benefits. The first is that the incoming threat is not merely sent in another direction, but is eliminated completely, so there will be no suprises that may arise as a result of only deflecting the threat. The second is that when the engulfed threat is dissipated, its energy goes to feed the shield itself, thus the more threats it is able to absorb, the more powerful it will become. This will allow, as the conflict continues, the user of the membrane shield to use personal energy for other purposes, as the shield itself is feeding off the efforts of the enemy.

    The ways around shields are just as infinite as the types of shields. Again, much of the way in which a practitioner will get around a shield depends upon that practitioner's visualization of the opponent's shield. If the shield is of the force field sort, a constant 'recalibration' of the attacks used may be able to stay one step ahead of the shield long enough to slip something through. Perhaps the practitioner could visualize the shield as the firewall software of a computer, and 'hack' the shield in order to bypass its defense grid and gain access to the 'mainframe', which would be the now unshielded practitioner behind the grid. If the shield is of the membrane style, then perhaps sending sizable attacks or a multitude of them could overload the absorption capacity of the shield. The more devious attacker could create a threat designed to destroy the shield from the inside, like an organic 'virus' the threat is absorbed by the shield, only to replicate and overload the shield from the inside. Naturally, there are several ways to bypass the need for complex shield-busting. One is to simply send such a powerful attack that the opponent's shield is not able to affect it, and is simply blown through as the threat makes it's way to the target. Another way is to plant an item on the person of the target, like a seemingly innocent gift of jewelry or perhaps a talisman slipped into their coat pocket when no one is looking. This item, given that it is connected to the attacker and according to the magical principle of contagion, provides the attacker with a way of instantly bypassing or corroding a breach in their target's shield. This is of course only two examples, as an infinite number of shields exist, as to the ways in which to neutralize their defenses.

Now that the concept of shielding has been explained, it would do to illustrate the practitioner's natural defenses. A practitioner, by virtue of being a dynamic magical being, has certain naturally occurring defenses. They work much like shields, and in essence can be visualized as naturally occurring shields, like the aura. Something that is simply a natural part of the physiology of a magus. Though, like the aura or muscle, the natural defenses can be strengthened through training. The best way to become more naturally shielded towards magical attacks is to actually be assaulted. Just like any martial artist will tell you, no amount of training beats actual experience. However, there are ways to train oneself so that the practitioner can survive those valuable experiences. The author and associates have developed a little exercise they have aptly named Spellblast. The concept is very simple, though its execution requires trust, control, and responsibility. The participants consciously lower their shields, and by powering down their defensive grids leave themselves open to magical assault. Then the participants cast very weak hexes at each other. By not being protected by their shields the participants take the full force of the hex, though because the hex is weak it is not overly damaging and its effects are temporary, the results being minor discomfort and misfortune. After being bombarded with these minor hexes the natural defenses are able to grow in potency and versatility as time goes on. Once the training is finished, shields are raised and the participants go through a cleansing to get rid of any persistent hex residue. After several years of this the natural defenses become quite potent, though constant evolution of the shields are also important. The end result is a practitioner with strong shields, though one who is capable of handling even powerful magical assaults when the shields are bypassed or if the practitioner is caught unawares.

Spell Trajectory

It is important when creating a sending (using magick), that the trajectory of the sending has been considered and incorporated into your work. The trajectory of a spell can be defined for this purpose as the path taken by the sending in order to achieve the intended results and manifestation of the practitioner's will. While this element of magical practice may seem elementary, the potency of the sending and its results can be increased exponentially if greater awareness and planning goes into the development of a trajectory.

While a great many spells seem to operate on a simple 'point A to point B' principle, the adept has the opportunity to further control and fine-tune the sending. Of course the most often used example is the ever popular money spell. If the caster does not specify where the money should come from and does not take steps in their own life to allow for a realistic gain in wealth, like look for a new job or play the lottery, then it is possible that the money may come due to reasons that are of negative consequence to the caster such as theft or the loss of a loved one.

Take for example this hypothetical situation: A magus wishing to place sigil graffiti underneath a public library in order to draw upon the knowledge energy patterns of the location decides to cast a spell of protection upon himself. At this point the spell is simply 'protection', which may manifest as the event going smoothly or the magus evading any unforeseen police responses. Though as a result of the unspecified nature of the spell, it may act to protect the magus from what could be a dangerous and illegal situation, and thus the magus finds himself bedridden with a broken leg or severe cold. While this is an extreme example, the possibilities of unintended results of an aspecific spell are indeed both positive and negative. The better, more specific approach to the spell, would be to cast a spell of protection against police intervention and a spell of 'It is my will for the mission to go smoothly'. By having the spell designed to empower the activity itself the magus has a greater chance of successfully tagging the building and escaping without notice. Though just in case, the magus has prepared a specific spell to use should the police discover his activities and attempt to arrest him for it. Should he decide that escape is preferable to arrest, then he has the spell at his disposal.

Like a hunter in the forest seeking your quarry, take care to visualize all of the possible outcomes of your shot before you take it. Take into account not only yourself and your target, but also the environment in which the sending will take place. By paying attention to environmental queues, situational factors, as well as the possible outcomes of the spell, the practitioner will be able to perceive and manipulate the path which their magick takes. Magick, like water for example, is most cases follows the path of least resistance. So by being aware of the situation, and attempting to visualize multiple outcomes and solutions, the magus will be able to best perceive what sort of sending to create and what path is best for the desired outcome. The more adept the practitioner becomes at this technique the more able he or she will be in developing effective trajectories in less and less amounts of time, so that potent sendings can still be cast should time ever be a factor.

Hot Spots

These are places of power, repositories or choke points of magical energy that can be tapped and harnessed for you own ends should you require magical energy in amounts beyond your personal capacity. Any place of cultural significance, social gathering, magical importance, or a waypoint of temporal travel. These could be churches, office buildings, nightclubs, sacred lands, or even a train station. Anywhere there is a constant flow of energy. With the right tech, a witch could utilize these hot spots to fuel her personal magick.

Let us begin with places of power, as they are the most obvious targets, even if the most uncommon. Places of power are just that, unique locations that seem to generate magical energy simply by existing, or as a result of their mystical significance. Some historical and well known examples of such locations could be the pyramids of Egypt, the stone temples of the Mayans, Stonehenge, the catacombs of Paris, or the temple mount in Jerusalem. Other lesser known hot spots are burial mounds, ancient forests, haunted buildings, or battlefields. There are also hot spots that can only be known on a local level or be perceived because of personal relevance. Examples of this would be the street mage who is empowered by a network of alleyways that, for him at least, seem to trace out a mystical pattern that generates magical energy. Or perhaps a practitioner that finds a particular country field to be sacred, for no other reason than that it has a potent magical resonance. The best way to interact with these sorts of hot spots is to simply be in their presence. While it is theoretically possible to subvert a place of power, to 'take control', the task is quite daunting and beyond the scope of this text. By being in the presence of these places of power the magus is able to allow himself to be permeated by the energies of the location. By drawing upon the ambient power of such locations, the magus can find a readily available source of 'free energy'. It should be noted however that the energy of such places carries with it a resonance similar to that of the location from which it springs forth. So it follows that power taken from a battlefield will have a more aggressive or sorrowful resonance, or power taken from a temple or holy place will take on the 'flavor' of the site.

Repositories are another sort of hot spot. Repositories differ from places of power in that the magical energy that resides within does not have its source in that particular location. Repositories are places where magical energy collects as a result of worship, energy sendings, or the symbolic meaning of the location. An example would be the various government buildings and national monuments in Washington D.C., the site of the Twin Towers tragedy in New York, Vatican City, or most any other place with cultural, religious, or national significance. There are other, lesser known but certainly powerful locations that are repositories. Such places as the houses owned by famous occultists, the hotel room in which Aleister Crowley dictated the Book of the Law, and the gravesite of Marie Leveau. Local hot spots can also act as repositories, there could be such energy reservoirs inside a famous college campus, a notoriously dangerous stretch of road, or a particularly popular nightclub. As to the methodology of pulling energy from such places is similar to the places of power in that simply being present within such locations is often sufficient to provide the needed energy. Though the application of runes or sigils designed to funnel energy into the magus are good ways to focus and control the flow of incoming energy. However, because these hot spots are not the sources of their own power, but receive it from outside sources, there is not the overriding need for restraint in the taking of energy from the location. While in a place of power the magick hungry magus might find that there are unsavory consequences that result from bleeding such a place dry to fuel his own desires. Though in a repository, due to its nature, can be used as much or as little as is needed. Regardless of the amount of energy drained, such a place receives its power because of its meaning and significance in the minds of the masses, and as such the magus would have to continually drain the location over a long period of time before any adverse effects began to arise. Though let it be said that discretion is a key skill for any sorcerer.

Choke points is a phrase that refers to any place, usually temporal, that acts as a waypoint in the general physical flow of the masses. Such places are focal points for the generally undirected energies of the masses. Potent examples would be massive train stations, highway toll booths, international airports, concert arenas, public beaches, amusement parks, shopping malls, and school campuses. People who are not practitioners of occult arts still generate plenty of energy, though unfocused, and generally broadcast it openly without perceiving their own energy fields. These choke points are the places in civilization that have the most dense gatherings of the unfocused masses, and thus are a rich miasma of free energy waiting to be harvested. As a result of this high concentration of ambient unfocused energy, there are very few ethical reprocutions from harvesting as much as is needed. The resonance of this energy is very weak due to the lack of focus, and as such is easily transmuted into useable magical energy that does not permeate the witch with a particular resonance in the way that a place of power or a repository will. The methodology of harvesting energy at choke points varies depending upon the specific location. For example, if a witch is trying to siphon power off of a crowd while at a concert, the best way would be for the witch to harvest the energy directly. That is to say that she could cast a spell directly on the crowd and siphon the energy directly from the ambient field generated by the crowd, or she might simply open her hand and call the energy to her. However, a sorcerer who wants to harness the human traffic at a local train station would be best served by using a sigil created for the purpose of collecting the energy of the passengers as they pass through the doors, ticket booth, or riding the train itself. The sorcerer could simply draw the sigil on a few stickers and paste them on walls, in doorways, or affix them to the ticket counter or turnstile. That way, each time someone enters the sigil's field of influence, it siphons off a miniscule amount of energy, and with hundreds of people passing it daily, the energy collects very quickly.

The discerning practitioner may find that drawing upon his or her own personal power is the most effective and rewarding source of energy. While this is indeed true, keep these alternative energy sources in mind. It is possible that in the course of your life that you may find yourself in a situation where having that extra juice can be the difference between success or failure, maybe even life or death.

Occult Machines

The creation and implementation of occult machines is a potent method of overcoming challenges in addition to making one's magical life somewhat easier. Like their more mundane counterparts, occult machines serve to allow the sorcerer to accomplish feats and complete tasks with more consistency, speed, and economy of energy. Again, in a fashion similar to their mundane counterparts, by design occult machines empower the sorcerer to create very complex magical workings by performing multiple functions in simultaneously. While the machine performs a multitude of simple magical functions the sorcerer is free to focus full attention upon working with even more powerful and complex magicks, thus the machine allows the sorcerer to perform magical acts that are otherwise in most cases too difficult, complex, or taxing.

The fundamental difference between a mundane machine and an occult machine is that the occult machine is powered by magick, and its primary functions are magical processes. There is a distinction between tools and machines, in both the mundane and occult worlds. A person using a crowbar to lever open a locked door is considered to be using a tool. In the same way a magus using a wand to aid in the casting of a spell is also considered to be using a tool. Though a person using a satellite imaging system to explore our planet's surface is considered to be the using of a machine. Similarly, a person using a remote viewing helmet that has been outfitted with sigils, a loadstone monocle, and other augmentations to explore our planet's surface would be considered to be using an occult machine.

An occult machine, by its nature, is a device that is fueled by subtle energies in order to produce a specified result. In many ways occult machines are closely associated with other mundane devices in that they produce similar results to their counterparts, it is their input/output methods that make them decidedly occult. Take the afore mentioned satellite imaging system and the remote viewing helmet. They both allow the user to see visual representations of their intended targets. The satellite tech is fueled by electricity, while the remote viewing helmet is fueled by magical energy. Because the helmet's function is to focus magical energy towards remote viewing, the energy gains that resonance as it passes from the helmet to the wearer. Also the various occult augmentations like the sigils and loadstone monocle, perform basic magical tasks like scrying, empowerment, and auric scanning, the sorcerer is better able to concentrate on the much more difficult task of tightening the focus and resolution of the remote viewing images and impressions. Granted, there are enough differences that to compare these two machines too closely would become a pointless exercise. Though, to illustrate the point, they will be said to be similar. It should also be noted that there are a great many magical and mundane machines that have no counterpart or likeness amongst the other group of machines. So while the remote viewing helmet is similar to the satellite system, the Eloigning Clock, which will be discussed at length momentarily, has no known functional counterpart amongst mundane machines.

It has been stressed in other texts that personal relevance is of paramount importance in the practicing of magick. Occult machines, due to their technological nature, are to some degree one of the few exceptions to that guideline. The entire function of an occult machine is that it will work regardless of who is using it at the time. Naturally there are several factors involved in using an occult machine. One must have some idea what the machine's function is, have the magical capacity and knowledge to activate the machine and control its use, and be able to perceive its process and results. Again using the remote viewing helmet as an example, if one sorcerer was to create the helmet it would of course have been created as a machine very personally relevant for its creator, and would carry with it the creator's personal style and taste. Though all another sorcerer would have to do to use the helmet for their own purposes would be to perceive its primary purpose, which would be remote viewing. Then find out how to activate the machine, which would likely be empowering a sigil or some other such symbolic 'lock & key' mechanism. Then the user would have to have the ability to focus and infuse the machine with magical energy, then the sorcerer would be free to use the machine for its intended purpose. The only alteration the interloper would possibly need to make is to change any elements of the machine that would make it more personally relevant to themselves, though generally a machine is a machine. In that all cars work off of the same principle, so if one recognizes a machine as a car, despite some design differences, all cars are designed and function the same way. So it is with magical machines. What follows are two further examples of the author's own occult machines, the Witchengine and the Eloigning Clock, to serve as examples for the creation of future occult machines.

    The Witchengine is a multi-purpose occult machine that acts at once like a portable generator of magical energy and a resonance filter. The physical component of the Witchengine is a simple cube. Several exist in wood, some of stone, and others of etched metal. Close associates of the author possess spherical witchengines, and in the spirit of tactical magick, one has recently been constructed with the ever useful ouija board. There are several sigils that have been etched, burned, or painted onto the engine. These sigils act as input/output ports. One draws in ambient magical energy, then once the energy is gathered another sigil strips the magical resonance of the energy. The resonance of the energy cannot be removed without separating out some of the energy itself, so the portion of the energy that contains the resonance of the location in which the engine is being used is vented out of the engine and back into the environment by an exhaust port sigil. The remaining energy is funneled through one of two sigils depending upon what the engine is being used for. If the desired function is to act as a portable battery the engine stores the energy in a silo sigil, where it is held until the user required an extra magical charge. If the desired function is to channel additional power directly into the user, yet another sigil exists to pour the energy straight into the user. There is a sixth sigil that acts as a lock, preventing others from using the machine casually, and must be overcome before the engine can be used, this is the reason that the cube is such a convenient physical vessel for such a machine. This machine was created for the express purpose of allowing the user to draw upon the ambient energy of the environment without picking up the resonance of the location from which the energy was taken. The only resonance to travel into the user along with the energy is that of the witchengine itself, which is for the most part an extension of the individual user. So a sorcerer using a witchengine in a place of negativity could draw energy from the environment without being permeated by the negative resonance of the place. It is a way to use magical tech to overcome the natural order of reality.

The Eloigning Clock is a gateway and the key to that gateway. Its physical component is actually a painting, though one with a complex background. The Clock exists not only on the physical plane but also in the subtle realms beyond. Though in this world simply a painting, its cadaver is an ever moving spherical body of concave silver plates that oscillate around a centerpiece of smoky quartz, which has been polished and shaped into a sphere. Crescent shaped pendulums swing in opposite directions from two opposite ends of the sphere, attached by tight and thin wires to the core of the sphere. The user connects with the Clock's subtle body through focusing upon the painting. Once a connection has been established with the subtle body of the Eloigning Clock, the painting of course being the artist's physical representation of that subtle body, the user can interface with the Clock. The machine is capable of functioning as a device for scrying into the subtle realms as well as acting as a waypoint for the user undertaking next-level travel into the subtle realms of the multiverse.

Ouija Boards

Almost everyone involved with magick and the occult has played on a ouija board, or at least has seen one. Most people have an opinion about them, those opinions ranging from fervent belief, adamant denial, or the concession that there is 'something' about them. In much of society, at least western cultures, the ouija board carries with it very potent associations with obsession, madness, control, and deception. There is much skepticism and debate, both in the occult underground and society at large, about the nature, purpose, and value of these 'talking' boards. Regardless of your personal beliefs, unless those beliefs have you doing everything you can to avoid them, ouija boards can be made into very powerful magical devices. With the right augmentations and associations, an industrious and skilled practitioner could turn a ouija board into the equivalent of an occult laptop, capable of functioning as a portable ritual space, casting tool, astral gateway, and grimoire.

While the history of ouija boards is dubious at best, and is irrelevant to the creation of this magical device. What is important however, is the socio-cultural empowerment that the boards receive. Contemporary ouija boards, to the best estimation, began as a parlor game, and were marketed as such by the board game industry. Like tarot cards before them, ouija boards were powerful occult tools that became highly commercialized and sold to non-practitioners in high volumes. Again, like the divinations of tarot cards these boards could occasionally be used successfully by the ignorant, contacting entities of varying natures and opening gateways through which multiple levels of reality could merge. Though for the most part these boards either did not function as advertised, were manipulated by the users subconsciously, or were the method in which the gullible were duped by a light-fingered charlatan. Despite all of the horror stories that came from misuse, the disappointment from failure to establish communication, and the predations of charlatans the ouija boards are still in production today. Also, because of its colorful and notorious history, the ouija board still commands the attention, opinions, and therefore energies of many people. Like thought-forms, deities, and ideas these boards gain power from their continued production, use, and infamy. With so many people being in contact with these boards, they have the potential to become powerful tools for the practitioner.

The metaphor of an 'occult laptop' is being used as a visualization for the purpose of communicating the idea, though if the individual using the board finds another visualization to be more effective, by all means use that. The primary reasons for the laptop visualization is that the board lends itself to such a metaphor. The board is thin, lightweight, and portable, much like its mundane counterpart. Using the above spell protocol and occult machine techniques the board can be made into a multifunctional tool that can be used in much the same way as a laptop. The ouija board can be given an onboard energy processor, be used to store spells or protocols, can be used to 'connect' to the subtle realms of reality, and is a tool that one can carry in a backpack or by hand without inconvenience.

One of the features of the ouija board is that it is a portable ritual space. Because of the occult associations held by conceptual reality, the ouija board creates a magical field simply by existing. When a magus pulls out the board and places it herself she has not only created a magical field by using a ouija board, there is the additional empowerment because the intention of the placement of the ouija board was to create a ritual space. So there is not only the power of the intent of the magus, but the power of the board itself as dictated by consensual reality. Another feature of the board is that it can be used as a casting tool. Like a wand, dagger, candle, or any other common casting tool, a ouija board can be used as such. As when it is used as a portable ritual space, the associations held about the power of a ouija board can provide a significant energy source when the board is used to help the caster focus for the casting of a spell. Imagine how disconcerting it might be to an opponent, or significant in the mind of the caster and thus empowering, to lay one hand on the ouija board and point the other at the target.

The ouija board can also be used for what it was intended, as a gateway to the other levels of reality, a portal into the greater multiverse and the subtle realms. While most people use the board in the popular style, by placing hands onto the planchette and allowing an entity to communicate with them through the board, there are other options available to the sorcerer should he or she choose. Depending upon the skill and ability of the practitioner to take and endure journeys of the consciousness into the subtle realms (astral travel), the board can be used in a much more invasive manner. Depending upon the particular technique the individual practitioner uses to gain access to the subtle realms, by employing the ouija board into that routine the magus will gain the energy infusion from the power that the board carries with it in addition to the resonance the board already possesses as a gateway tool in pop-culture.

In addition to being a ritual space, casting tool and gateway, the ouija board can also be used as a grimoire. The magus can cast spells into the board, using it as a storage device. First the magus should cast the spell, then at the moment the spell is leaving the caster, target a specific point on the board, pushing your spell into the board itself. By choosing a specific location on the board, be it one of the letters, numbers, pictures, the yes or no, or the goodbye, the practitioner is able to trap the spell in progress. It should be mentioned at this point that the technique of managing the spell trajectory is very important, in that the spell hitting the board before the target is integral to the success of the spell storage. Once the spell is 'installed' onto the board, the practitioner can wait to use the spell at the most opportune moment. For example, an industrious magus may have several curses bound into the A, the 3, and the Goodbye. When the spells are needed, the magus 'activates' the spell through some personally relevant method (breathing onto the symbol, touching it with a finger, moving the planchette over it and saying a command word, etc), the spell in progress leaves it's stasis inside the board and continues on it path towards the target. In this way a sorcerer could conceivable carry an entire array of spells in progress that only need the touch of a symbol to activate, thus having the potential to cast a multitude of spells in a short amount of time given that the spells have already been cast, and only need to be released.

      Another method of using the board as a grimoire or casting devise is to associate each character or image on the board with a particular spell or magical concept. Much like sigil magick, the sorcerer could then mix and match the characters on the board (most likely touching them or using the planchette to activate them in the desired order) to create and cast whatever spell that is desired. Or the magus could simply empower the board to manifest his or her will according to the letters and numbers highlighted by the planchette, simply spelling out what the magus desires, and empowering the board to focus the will to achieve the desired result. The author and some of his associates choose to what they call 'hotwire' their ouija boards by placing stickers, painting, or drawing various sigils and magical symbols or phrases on the backs of their boards to further empower them on a personal level. This technique can also be used to setup wards to prevent other practitioners or entities from taking over the board and using it to their own ends. The use of ouija boards in magical practice can be both effective and stylish.

Subverting Reality

Consensual reality, in most cases, is acutely opposed to the practice of real magick. Practitioners come to find that their entire lives are a constant struggle against the forces of doubt, persecution, and the devaluing of their chosen path in life. Our society, government, and educations are all in conflict with what we as magi know to be true, magick works. Because of this indoctrination and conditioning practitioners are always having relapses into doubt, questioning their sanity, and becoming conflicted with what their familial, professional, and educational influences would have them believe. While this is an almost unavoidable lifelong struggle, there are ways to temporarily bypass this wall of denial and create effective magical manifestations. The most potent of these will be discussed here, which is in essence 'playing reality's game'.

Consensual reality, while not at all concrete, can be made to work for the warlock instead of against him. Within consensual reality there are many superstitions, cultural attachments, and associations that can be used to empower an act of magick that is done 'according to the rules'. While indeed a mage is a dynamic force of change, sometimes it is less difficult and more effective to operate within the boundaries of established reality. For example, as with the ouija board mentioned above, most people generally believe (when they don't think anyone is looking) that 'black magick' done to the photograph of a person will work. Even if they say they don't, even the most atheistic person will get at least a little unnerved if they were to discover that someone had taken a picture of them and stabbed it full of holes.

The point is, if a magus works magick within these 'boundaries' of consensual reality, it will actually help to support the actions taken by the magus. This is where the benefits of Aleister Crowley's "Live like a Magician" philosophy become much more apparent. Its risky admittedly, but if one were to adopt the 'style' of what consensual reality erroneously believes to be how a mage is supposed to be, then magick within those boundaries becomes much easier to manifest. For example, consensual reality rejects the existence of a man in a three piece suit standing on top of a sigil holding a dead chicken and a rainstick. However, consensual reality does seem to allow for the possibility that a Hopi shaman could speak with the spirits of the land through a vision quest. Similarly, consensual reality rejects the idea that a exorcism could be performed by a goth witch on a possessed child using a teddy bear to bind the malignant spirit. Though that same reality allows for the possibility that a Catholic priest could accomplish the same task with the Lord's prayer and a bible. It's a question of style and perception.

While this may not work for some practitioners, those who find themselves in need of a break from the constant struggle with consensual reality may find that by playing the 'part of the magus' may actually provide some relief and yield useful magical results. In this case, conformity may be the backdoor you have been looking for. Simply identify those elements of magick that seem to be a part of culture, social association, or superstition and exploit them. Who knows, maybe the more magick we incorporate into our personal style and daily lives the more consensual reality will adapt.

Crisis Energy

Just as every spell is affected by the resonance of the magical energy that fuels it, so can the resonance of the energy and resulting spell be affected by the situation in which the event occurs. It has been established that magical energy has the resonance of locations, and that spells can resonate within the magus who casts them. Yet the power of a situation can also affect both the resonance of the energy and spell, but also the potency. One element of this concept of situational influences on magick that will be investigated here is Crisis Energy.

For the purpose of this topic, crisis will be defined as the moment of intense transformation of one state of being into another. For example, a piece of chalk sitting on the palm of someone's hand is considered in general, all quantum physics aside, to be in a state of rest, otherwise a state of potential. If that someone dropped the piece of chalk it would be in motion, or in a kinetic state. The minute moment of time in which the chalk has been released from its state of potential but has yet to become kinetic is a time when the chalk is in a state of crisis.

When applied to magic the idea of crisis becomes a potent, if at times volatile, source of energy and gnosis. The concept of crisis energy, when applied to magical practice, becomes the moment in a sorcerer's life when immediate action must be taken to resolve a situation. These moments of crisis exist right before an automobile accident but after it is inevitable, in that state of crisis the magus has the opportunity to change reality and alter the situation. By identifying when these moments happen, the adept can in effect 'alter fate'. The auto accident is narrowly avoided as the magus identifies the moment of crisis and utters the word 'no', then miraculously avoids the accident entirely.

Crisis magick occurs when the bullet IS going to hit you, but then you become empowered by that moment of crisis, and with your magical will deny the bullet its rightful target.

It is the moment of clarity in which your magick MUST work. The mastery of crisis energy is the result of observing the moments in one's daily life in which a state of crisis is achieved by objects, ideas, or people. The more adept as identifying and tapping the crisis energy, the more you will be able to direct the outcomes of the events in your life. Oddly enough, the power of crisis magick works in reverse to most other methods of magick in that the ability to affect the smaller, more minute details of life is the mark of the master, while altering the outcomes of important events is in general the less difficult task. It is easier to identify and tap the crisis energy of a life and death situation than it is in a more routine or daily occurrence. That is not to say that avoiding bullets and car crashes is easy, far from it, yet in such dire circumstances the extraordinary is much more likely to occur. Though it is to say that it is much more difficult, and requires much more skill, will, and ability to stop objects from falling, prevent a car from starting, or altering the trajectory of a thrown object.

While crisis theory can be used as infrequently as only to alter traumatic events or as often as to attempt to control the outcomes of many daily occurrences or perhaps even the attempt to manifest a sort of functional telekinesis (possible if unlikely). The most practical use of crisis energy is in the application of daily magick. Before casting the spell, become aware that there will be a time in the casting in which the spell will either succeed or fail, then use your will to empower the spell to further success. By becoming aware of the event horizon between do or do not, you can use the state of crisis to gain the gnosis required to achieve the outcome you desire.

Omnimancy

There is a trend in both literature and practice to affix labels to particular styles or magical systems in order to distinguish them as valid paths or concepts within an occult context. The benefit of this methodology of classification is that once a technique or system of magick has been identified and labeled, it becomes concrete and definable, something that can be studied and learned in an at least superficially ordered manner. In many ways once such a classification occurs a style can emerge, and a system built upon it, then perhaps even a personal paradigm can be created using the style of magic as a way of interacting with reality. Take necromancy for example, at its core a magical style that utilizes the multifaceted energies, entities, and concepts of death, the dead, and dying. When one begins to layer upon that basic style the beliefs, practices, rituals, and formulas of an individual or group that is focused upon this style, it can evolve into a functioning magical system. Once that magical system becomes the primary mode of interaction with reality, it has the potential to become a personal paradigm.

The purpose of this chapter is to show that by simply adding the suffixes 'mancy' and 'mancer' to certain words, actions, and ideas, the industrious practitioner could use these linguistic labels to spontaneously generate fully functional magical systems with a fusion of language and logic. By becoming adept at identifying opportunities for generating these systems within the practitioner's daily life, that person would potentially have a plethora of magical systems on hand in order to resolve any situation or desire that may arise. For example, in this way a practitioner is able to not just cast a spell using death energies, but is able to do so in that specific moment as a full fledged necromancer. Then once the spell has been cast return to the original resonance of the practitioner. This technique will allow the practitioner to become a much more potent and dynamic magus, able to do magick at any given moment from any magical system as if the practitioner was fully immersed in that system. A person who has mastered this technique can go from being one sort of magus to being a different sort, and be genuine in the transition, then return to the original form once the moment has passed. The best description of this magical system, for what else could it be but a style or system, is Omnimancy. The practitioner who utilizes the full spectrum of magical applications is an Omnimancer. Though in each individual act of magick the practitioner may be a necromancer, pyromancer, technomancer, or a multitude of possibilities, the fundamental mutable system is Omnimancy (which of course is also a paradigm to be used and discarded as needed, just like any other).

It is likely that the reader at this point is aware of some of the more common systems of necromancy (death), oneiromancy (dreams), chiromancy (palmistry), technomancy (technology), and many other more common sorts of magical systems. What follows are several examples, some more unorthodox than others, that will serve to illustrate the grand spectrum of magick available to a practitioner wishing to utilize omnimancy. Always remember that a magus can, with diligence and sincerity, conceivably be a 'mancer' of just about anything, though naturally some 'mancies' will be more useful and easier to work with than others.

Urbanomancy- The urbanomancer is a magus who is attuned to the resonance of the city. They strive to become aware of the ebb and flow of city life, traffic, public opinion, and the general state of affairs in their environment. Where someone else may find a subway commute tedious and draining, the urbanomancer is able to draw vitality from such a journey. They are able to navigate the cityscape and avoid unpleasant encounters, which in most ways is how their magick manifests. (A useful system in a traffic jam or on a crowded subway).

Bibliomancy- Book magick and information magick. This is the power of divination and of control. The bibliomancer is able to divine knowledge, precognition, and gnosis from techniques such as automatic writing, random Internet searches, sporadic reading of text, and barely perceivable patterns in text or data. The bibliomancer is also able to manipulate these elements, making information difficult or easy to find, arranging for ideas to spring forth into the collective subconscious, and many other possible applications of their attunement to information. (This is a system that is very useful for research or study, or making certain information disappear.)

Pornomancy- The pornomancers, called so in order to distinguish what they do from neo-pagan sex magic, are adepts of sex, gender, sexuality and the energies surrounding them. There is a great deal of energy generated from sexual encounters, though pornomancers are able to, unlike some other magical systems, gain gnosis without requiring the magical participation of their partner. For a pornomancer, casual sex and one night stands can be just as empowering as intense ceremonial encounters or actual lovemaking. Also, they are able to generate and manipulate the energy from sexuality and eroticism. Naturally most pornomancy takes the form of carnal encounters or magick based in physicality. (Good for getting laid, and snatching up some gnosis along the way.)

Neuromancy- Neuromancers are magi who have successfully integrated the theory of neuro-linguistic programming into a magical system. They are able to combine magick and memes with their knowledge of human behavior, socio-cultural conditioning, symbology, subterfuge, and personal charisma to impose their will upon the people around them. While neuromancy requires a significant amount of academic study and magical prowess, it is a very powerful system. (Making people do and think what you want them to.)

Magical Combat

Most magi at some point in their careers are forced to participate in magical conflicts. These conflicts can occur for a multitude of reasons and be fought on many different levels. The author has previously published a text on the planning, adaptation, and execution of such conflicts in a separate work, titled The Occult Art of War. However, this chapter will go into detail about the tactics and methods of participating in these conflicts. While magical violence is a topic that is often preceded by disclaimers and exhaustive essays on the law of returns, karma, and the moralities of such actions, this chapter will deal explicitly with hex creation, countermagick, and offensive augmentation. Let is be said now that it is the opinion of the author that magick itself is amoral, and it is the individual who uses magick that is ultimately responsible.

The hex, or curse, is the name that will be ascribed to any sort of offensive magick in this chapter. While there are many ways in which to magically assault an opponent, several will be detailed here. A hex, at its core, is a spell designed to influence the life of the target in a negative manner, to manifest the will of the attacker in the form of injury, misfortune, sickness, and death. This damage can occur on multiple levels, the two most common are etheric and physical. The etheric is the layer of reality that is most similar and approximate to physical reality. While it is a subtle realm, it is closely tied to the physical, and changes wrought in that reality directly affect the physical. For example, if a magus was to lay a curse upon the spiritual corpus (subtle body that exists in the subtle realms) of an opponent, that cursed person would find that curse manifesting on an etheric level. The most common signs of damage that occurs as a result of etheric assault are sudden bouts of depression, anxiety, suicidal thoughts, or self-destructive behaviors and severe mental disorders for which there are no physiological explanations. Horrible nightmares, sleeping disorders, night terrors, and hallucinations are also signs of etheric trauma. The physical layer of reality needs no explanation, as it is the realm in which humanity spends the majority of its consciousness enmeshed within. A hex that is cast upon the physical corpus of a target tends to have much more physically damaging effects, and thus is more difficult to cast successfully because of the internal layers of doubt held by most magi that their spells can be so powerful. However, if the practitioner can overcome this illusory limitation and accept that magick can exist and affect the physical world, then such spells can be severe and effective. Physical hexes tend to manifest as financial, relationship, or professional misfortune in addition to sudden illness, unexplained or coincidental injury, and possibly death. More often than not such physical occurrences seem to the untrained eye as coincidence or freak occurrence, and are usually not attributed to a hex.

Hexes, or curses by another name, exist in an infinite variety. The magus who is more oriented towards traditional styles and traditions of magical practice can find a wide variety of offensive magick in the annals of history, mythology, and tribal culture. Such sources are full of curses and hexes. From the black corn curse of the Hopi, the voodoo dolls of the Afro-Caribbean cultures, the demon bowls of Babylon, and (when hurling it at someone perceived as demon or heretic) the Lord's prayer of the Catholic faith. Though history, culture, and mythology are not the only sources of hexes. As a modern magus the practitioner has the opportunity to borrow from these cultural spells as he or she chooses, mixing and matching to fit the occasion. Also, the practitioner doesn't even need to have elements of these tried and true methods in order to make a hex work. All that is needed is a clear intent to do harm and the focus/power sufficient to manifest these changes in reality according to one's will. Often the magus will need ritual or ceremonial elements to the spell for the purpose of providing the magus with a method for focusing on the spell with the intensity as is required to manifest such results. So any ritual, ceremonial, or physical component that is personally relevant to the individual caster can be used. For example, three magi wish to curse the same individual. One magus may choose to create a painting of the individual suffering the effects of the curse, then burn the painting as a way of sending the curse to its target. The second magus may opt to write the hex on a piece of sturdy parchment paper, empower the paper with inked curse sigils, and bury the paper somewhere near the target's home, school, or job. The third magus may simply meditate and listen to a particularly violent piece of music while focusing their attention on 'wishing ill' to the target. Usually a hex is designed to affect the target on either the etheric or the physical level of reality. Though assaulting the target on both levels is possible.

Should the magical senses of the victim or the victim's associates be sufficiently acute, countermagick can be attempted. Like hexes, most countermagick works on the etheric level, physical level, or both simultaneously (much more difficult). Countermagick is magick that targets the spells and magical workings of other practitioners or entities. While countermagick has its applications outside the realm of hex removal, the methods in which countermagick is employed to resolve curses are the same methods used to perform countermagick in most any capacity, so as the technique remains similar, only the combat aspect will be dealt with in this chapter.

The most effective form of countermagick is to have potent shielding techniques as described above. If one's shields are of sufficient versatility and power, they can resolve most incoming magical assaults before their negative influence can infect the life of the magus being assaulted. Should the shields be circumvented for whatever reason, there are several techniques for removing unwanted magical influences. One method is to construct magical countermeasures that extend beyond simple shielding. Creating talismans, wards, or spells that are specifically designed to block, absorb, dissipate, redirect, or reflect incoming offensive spells are a very effective method. The best way to accomplish this is to create the spell with much the same technique and visualizations as one creates shields, then once the core spell has been constructed, load a 'defense' protocol into the spell. By visualizing how the spell will function and the sorts of magical influences it will guard against as you create it will further empower the spell to your advantage.

Inevitably there will be offensive magicks that will slip past the defenses of any magus, just as entropy enters any physical system, so will harmful magick eventually find its way into the life of every practitioner at some point in their lives. When this occurs the best way of dealing with those magical influences is what will be could the 'scorched earth' method. First isolate the target of the spell, be it a person, building, beast, or object. The goal is to blast the victim with an overwhelming amount of magical energy with the intent of removing any and all magical influences. While this method will also remove positive magical influences, this is a good way to be absolutely sure that the negative influences have been removed, as most such spells are very insidious and difficult to completely root out any other way. This can be done entirely by direct energy manipulation without any ritual component should the victim and associates choose. Though some ritual components are usually helpful. Perhaps the magus could draw a bath of hot water and scented oils and 'soak away' the harmful influences. A trip to a bath house or a sweat lodge is an effective way of leeching out the offensive magick, provided that the actions taken are sufficiently empowered by the will of the practitioner. For buildings a good method is to redecorate, remodel, or freshly paint the property. Items can be dipped, sprinkled, or sprayed with empowered 'magical cleansing solution' and left to dry or rest in a sufficiently empowered location for a period of time. The author and associates (when not using the pure energy method) have at times used 'decontamination chambers', which are simply temporary ritual spaces created through placing sigils on every window and door of a room, then having the victim remain in the room inside a sigilized 'detox' casting circle for varying lengths of time.

Magical offensive augmentations is another method of magical combat. This technique is the use of magick to augment pre-existing forms and tools of conflict. While this element of magical violence is not usually a part of the life of many magi, there is always the chance of a situation requiring such techniques and activities. For people who practice magick as more of a hobby or pastime, this is an element of magick that may not become of any precedence. Though for those of us who have incorporated magick into our daily lives, we have the opportunity to use it in ways that many others have no occasion to attempt. We will discuss several sorts of offensive augmentations, the use of magick to empower mundane tools to be effective on an etheric level, and the ability to lay magick aside in favor of more effective methods.

As modern magi we have access to a great many tools of conflict. The techniques described can be used in conjunction with any tool, though for the confines of this chapter we will discuss the gun, the knife, and the fist. As they are the most preeminent tools of violence in modern society, they hold a special place in the magical arsenal of a magus. It is hoped that one will never have to use such tools, though preparedness is a key element of magical practice, and as such these tools are a part of the sorcerer's toolbox.

While no amount of magical enhancement can replace technical skill with a firearm, an industrious magus can use sigils and spells to increase the accuracy of the firearm and enable the bullets to cause harm on an etheric level as well. Let it be stated that while firearms can be made, through magical augmentation, to harm non-physical entities, the physical bullets must still be accounted for, and so the use of firearms for this pursuit is discouraged. There are two common ways to empower a firearm with magick. One way is to use a metal engraving tool to etch sigils of accuracy and etheric harm into the gun itself, or if one is careful the bullet casings (don't blow yourself up by pressing too hard). The other is to empower the gun before shooting, usually by calmly blowing a controlled breath into the gun (usually into the firing mechanism or the trigger, don't blow your head off blowing down the barrel). The breath acts as a carrier for the magical energy that fuses with the gun to make it more damaging and accurate.

The knife can be similarly empowered, by etching sigils of harm and striking precision onto the blade or handle. Also, like the gun, a knife can be 'awakened' with the breath or some other significant act. Unlike the firearm, the knife is a most effective tool for dealing with non-physical entities, as they can be struck and damaged without much risk of the injury of bystanders or property. Again, this is a situation in which the possession of acute magical senses is of vital importance. With a blade that 'works both ways', a magus can enter almost any location without fear of not being able to defend themselves. Most entities will flee the sight of a witch carrying an enchanted blade and prepared to use it for real. Using a knife against a live opponent is a different matter all together. There are many books and classes available to teach one how to properly use and care for a knife, and it is highly suggested that such training is undertaken as soon as possible. As with the gun, there is an overwhelming temptation to use the knife as a tool of prevention instead of a tool of resolution, this is a mistake. As many of the training manuals and live instructors will tell you, never draw a weapon that you do not have the will or intention of using.

For those readers who have ever trained in martial arts, the idea of using magick in conjunction with physical combat is not an new idea. For those who have not, it is possible to blend magical technique with physical combat in such a way as to make the body of the mage a casting tool. It is suggested that training manuals or classes with live instructors be consulted on the actual technique of physical combat, as there are many styles of martial arts available and the style that best suits your personal needs is out there somewhere. The blending, once a rudimentary understanding of a martial style is achieved, of magick and physical combat results in the ability to harm the subtle bodies of the opponent. In essence, the ability to harm someone's 'soul' with physical techniques. By becoming aware of the energy fields generated by the physical body, and developing an awareness of the etheric realm and resulting spiritual corpus of the energy, the magus can produce results far beyond those possible by non-practitioner combatants.

For example, one magus, though no fault of his own, becomes involved in a late night bar fight. He avoids a clumsy strike from his assailant and delivers a powerful fist strike to the abdomen of his attacker. The fight is broken up and everyone goes home. The assailant is not even bruised where he was struck, but soon develops severe internal damage in the form of a bleeding ulcer because his etheric subtle body was torn to shreds the night before when struck by the magus. While this may seem like an extreme example, it is not. Extreme would be causing aneurysms and cardiac arrest. As most energy healers and mystics will tell you, severe damage to the subtle bodies results in some pretty heinous physical manifestations.

The final form of magical combat is the ability to leave magick behind and consider other options. On one level, this is the ability to blend mundane skills with magical technique. If a witch has constructed a curse statue, she must have the stealth and intelligence to bury the statue in the backyard of her target without being noticed, which is a difficult task indeed. Though on a more meaningful level, the ability to leave magick behind is manifested in the magus being able to find alternative solutions to magick. Sometimes the best way to get someone to like you is to talk to them, while magick can help, it must be provided with avenues in which to manifest. While a spell for a new career is a powerful thing, one must actually go out and look for a new job. Though this chapter is about violence, so in closing an example of magical combat without magick will be used. Let's say that you have just entered into magical combat with an opponent who is far more powerful than yourself, and the offensive magick being hurled against you is far more than you can handle. Your magick seems to just bounce off the shields of your opponent, and nothing you can do magically seems to make any difference. If magick isn't working, try something more mundane. If you are wealthy, buy their house note from the bank and evict. If you are a computer whiz you could alter vital information. There are many ways in which you can resolve your magical violence situation other than magick. Think about this, how different would the occult community be if in their famous magical battle S.L. Mathers, who was clearly outmatched by Aleister Crowley, had put aside magick and instead leaned across the table and punched Crowley in the teeth? Hard to 'do as thou wilt' when choking on your own blood.

Magick by Rote

While the primary focus of this book is to show that magick can be created from scratch, and no specific formula must be followed to achieve results, this chapter will illustrate the advantage of keeping track of these patchwork magical creations. When a magus discoveres a particular combination of components that are effective at creating the desired manifestation, that magus could benefit on a personal level by recording this event. There are a great many occult texts that encourage the reader to keep a magical diary or journal, this book is no different. Though it may seem tedious and will initially be difficult to form the habit, once this act becomes second nature the magi will be able to track his or her own progress through the pages of this diary. Over time the sorcerer will be able to recognize patterns in his magick, and be able to extract further knowledge and technique from his own writings as if he were being his own teacher. Not only will this diary allow the sorcerer to observe personal progress, he will be able to create what will be called 'rotes'.

Rote is just a fancy word for a specific magical technique that produces results worth repeating. If a witch casts a particular spell, making it up as she goes, and is pleased with the results, she may choose to use the same procedure in a future situation. Despite the knowledge that ritual and procedure are simply methods in which to focus the will of the magus, one can use these procedures over and over again if they produce the desired results. That is the whole point of tactical magick, use what works. So if you discover that casting a spell using specific ritual, physical, and verbal components is producing the desired results, why not repeat the procedure? By keeping a magical diary you will be able to search it for these similarities, and in so doing end up compiling your own list of rotes. This list of rotes will become your personal grimoire, the foundation of your own tradition. As time goes on your grimoire will grow until you have a fully functioning magical system of your own making, and while it is personally relevant, may even be of use to others. Naturally the magus will still end up using improvised magick and eclectic techniques for much of their magical lives, though by having rotes at your disposal you have systematic magick with predictable results should you need it.

For those who have read the author's previous texts this chapter on rotes should illustrate the methods used to develop the more formulaic and stylish spells presented in those earlier texts. For those new to the concept, the following example rotes have been provided, each with its own unique (and creative) title, description, and components.

Denial- This spell is an act of countermagick to be used when the magus is able to perceive an oncoming magical assault. By calling up a countermagick sigil through visualization, the magus projects the sigil towards the offensive magick. When the sigil comes in contact with the assault, depending upon the style of countermagick, it will deflect, absorb, or reflect the magical assault.

Components- The magus may choose to create the sigil in written form on parchment and commit it to memory. Once it is firmly in the memory, empower and burn the parchment into ashes, visualizing the burning of the parchment as the commitment of the sigil into magical reality. Then, if consuming those ashes is a personally relevant act, do so. When calling up the sigil the magus may choose to breathe it towards its target or to 'hurl' it with a hand gesture or power word.

Spirit Nuke- This spell is designed to allow the magus to remove all magical influences (be they spell or entity) from a particular area. A container, full of magical ingredients, is infused with as much magical energy as the magus is able to harness three times a day for three days. This timetable is based upon the mystical significance of 3, though any numerically significant timetable can be used depending upon the individual magus. As the container is being filled with magical energy for the allotted time, bind runes are placed on the container to prevent the energy from dissipating prematurely. Then the container is taken to the target area and placed at the closest approximation of the center. A protective circle or ward sigil is drawn under or around the container, to prevent unwanted tampering or premature release of the spell. Depending upon what sort of activation protocol the magus has constructed for the container, this protocol is employed and the nuke 'detonates'. It will release the stored energy in one massive blast, the energy naturally having been placing into the container with the intent to 'drive out' all magical influences and thus resonating with that purpose. Take care not to be too close to the 'blast radius' of the container, as nearby magi could suffer severe etheric damage from the spell.

Components- The container can be anything that makes the participating magi think 'bomb', this could be a shoebox, tin can, garbage pail, or plastic cylinder of some kind. The author and associates prefer to use a perforated cardboard cylinder (for reasons illustrated below). The type of material in the container should be materials that, at least in the minds of the participating magi, cause harm or distress to magical entities. The author and associates have used large amounts of salt, mixed with a vial of iron filings and a diced garlic clove. The bind runes are simply magical symbols designed to keep the energy contained until the nuke is ready to be deployed. Symbols of personal design are certainly effective, as are any symbols, sigils, or runes that are of personal relevance to the participating magi. The author and associates prefer to use bind runes of their own make. The activation protocol is also a very flexible element of the nuke's construction. Spell protocols (as mentioned in previous chapters) can be loaded into the device, allowing for a remote magical 'detonation'. Or the magi can make the device 'breath activated', so that the magus breathes the activation power into the nuke, then makes a run for it as the power unlocks the bind runes and touches off the blast. For those of a more, alternative, mindset, there is the option of actual explosives. The author and associates have in the past used a various combination of over-the-counter fireworks to spice up the rote. When the fuse is lit and the device explodes it sends the mixture of salt, iron, and garlic outwards into the target area (hence the use of cardboard, shrapnel is counterproductive). Granted the target area smells like garlic for a few days, spiritual radiation perhaps, but it 'works like a charm'.

Working with a Group

There are several types of group practice available to the discerning magus. There are the close-knit covens, international magical societies, and a multitude of groups of every size in between. It is important to examine both the group and your personal reasons for wishing inclusion within that group. The benefits must be weighted against the hindrances to your personal magical development and practice.

Covens, as such groups will be called in this chapter, tend to be small groups of between five and twelve people that have no allegiance to groups outside of the local coven. Covens are very polarized in their lifespan in that they either exist for only a few short months or years while others last for the lifetime of those involved. Groups like this are powerful in that they are usually all friends or at least associates outside the confines of the coven, though this can at times be a disadvantage. When friendships or relationships within the coven and social group go sour, there can be severe magical consequences. Another disadvantage is that some covens have members that are romantically entangled with one or more of the members, and often the maturity and social boundaries of the coven are strained or broken when romantic tensions reach their peak. However, because of the intimate nature of covens the members can expect a great deal more emotional, magical, and physical support from the coven than most other magical groups. Most covens are unified by a particular magical system or set of beliefs, though often the interpretation of these beliefs gives the coven a strong diversity in actual magical application. Group casting also tend to be a favored activity of such groups. Conflicts within the group on a magical level are much less protracted than in larger groups and are resolved much more quickly, though these conflicts tend to be much more intense given that the average coven is enmeshed within the social and physical circles of the members. Many covens are centralized around a particular location, which is most often a residence which houses one or more of the coven members.

Large magical societies also have their unique advantages and disadvantages. The primary strength of international societies is that the members often have a network of contacts throughout the world, and can reach other members through various official channels. In addition to a vast support network, the members share a common set of beliefs and magical practice, with each member in the society ascribing to the same, in general, magical system. The disadvantages of such groups spring forth from their very strengths. Magical societies are so vast and virulent precisely because of their common vision of reality, and typically require various oaths, bindings, and financial obligations in addition to an at times strict adherence to certain beliefs or methods. Often such groups have an organizing document, charismatic leader, or meta-narrative that binds the group together with a common paradigm, magical system, and code of behavior. While this is advantageous for those practitioners who thrive on group work and magical doctrine, other more independent minded individuals may be stifled in such an environment.

The above examples are of the small intimate groups and the large and at times impersonal international societies. There exist in the world many groups of varying sizes, with many being groups that resemble covens in that they are unified by social ties and more intimate magical relations though have several dozen members. There are also international magical societies that have a worldwide membership in name only, and the society is made up of individuals with not real social network. There are schools and lecture centers, workshops and temples, and all manner of group dynamics spread across the globe. What is important is for the individual practitioner to decide what he or she needs out of a group, then choose accordingly.

In the spiritual community, and to some degree the occult community, there is an alarming number of charlatans and manipulators. It is important not to fall in with these sorts of groups, as they hinder both social and magical growth, perhaps even becoming abusive or dangerous. There are many sources available for research into the subject of cults and the negative aspects of group work. The author is not an expert on cults, and highly suggests that the reader to independent research into abusive groups in order to gain a working knowledge of such groups. It is up to the individual practitioner to be observant, keeping watch for the warning signs of cult indoctrination, the predations of the group leadership, and harmful doctrines or adherence to dogma that may hinder the growth of the individual practitioner. Never fall victim to fear or peer pressure, be prepared to shoot your way out if you have to, and you'll be fine. That said, there are several warning signs specifically for, but not limited to, occult groups that need to be taken into consideration.

Charismatic leaders are to be automatically viewed with suspicion. Men and women who lead their groups by force of personality, personal charm, or reputed magical power. For example, if you are invited to join a coven in which members believe that they receive their magical potency directly from the group's leader, stay away. This simply becomes a vehicle for control, with the leader having the 'power' to take magical potency away from members. Groups that have leaders who 'channel' otherworldly beings or forces, then encourage the group to live by the proclamations or teaching of that being are to be regarded with skepticism. It is possible that the leader is either a charlatan and not channeling anything but his or her own ego, or perhaps the entity being channeled is not what it says it is or is manipulating the group through the leader. Basically any group that has a leader who relies upon his or her personal abilities instead of their knowledge or teachings and who does not encourage critical thinking is not to be trusted. Certainly join if you choose, but be ready to get out if things get dodgy.

Magical dogma is also to be approached with reservation. Most sufficiently developed magi have come to understand that there are a multitude of way of practicing magick, though others may work better than some, there is a healthy current of diversity in most modern magi. If you come into contact with a group that encourages indoctrination into a specific magical system to the exclusion of others as a way of devaluing other paths, this group may stifle your creativity and individual magical development. It is much like going to a martial arts school and having the teacher try to claim that the style taught by their school is the only way to beat ass. Its just not true. If they have elements to their magical system that you wish to learn in order to incorporate, then by all means do join. Though understand that as you progress others in the group may take notice that you have infiltrated their group without total adherence to their beliefs, and conflict may result.

The final warning sign, though while on occasion applies to men, is focused as a warning for women. There is a strong undercurrent of sexual predation within spiritual communities, healing communities, and especially in occult circles. While this is most prevalent in smaller coven sized groups, there are predators lurking in the ranks of the larger international groups. They have several tactics for engaging in their abuse. If you find yourself approached by an all male coven for membership, be cautious. If you find yourself invited to a ceremony or ritual in the role of 'goddess', be skeptical. There are groups out there that will use the lure of magick and witchcraft as a way of pulling in females who are interested in occult practice. Once involved the unwary female is often targeted by one or more of the male members, and after its too late she realizes that she was invited to participate as a way of getting her sexually involved with one or more of the members of the group and not from a recognition of her magical potential or value. Its like a very complex pick-up line. If some guy is trying to get you to let him 'teach you magick', listen to your bullshit alarm when it goes off. Though most sexual abuse occurs in smaller covens, international societies have their own breed of predators. These are the members who joined the society because they believe that 'loose' women also join such organizations. These self-styled 'magi' are nothing more than sexual predators looking for an easy lay.

The purpose of this chapter is not to instill a sense of paranoia or to dissuade the reader from joining a magical group, quite the opposite. Having been involved in both covens and international societies, the author has witnessed much of what is mentioned above. Cult influence can be neutralized. Sexual predators can be avoided. Magical indoctrination can be guarded against. The purpose of this chapter is to encourage individual practitioners to exercise common sense, caution, and awareness of the situations in which they find themselves. The benefits of group practice can be worth the risk, as long as they are pursuant to the manifestation of your will.

The Toolbox

An important aspect of tactical magick is the sorcerer's toolbox. This can be an actual container or a metaphorical description of the sorcerer's collection of magical tools and components. The toolbox is the source from which the practitioner draws the various materials and elements of his or her magical workings. Naturally the more personally relevant the materials the magus gathers, the more potent the results of the magical endeavors. Though the variety of the materials is also important, as to provide a material flexibility when working magick in the vast spectrum of situations in which the practitioner may find a use for magical workings.

For example, a magus could take a container that has some personal significance (perhaps an old heirloom trunk or a handmade wooden chest), and place upon it sigils of creativity, inspiration, or whatever else is seen as advantageous. Then inside the toolbox there are magical items of personal relevance: perhaps a few vials of essential oils, incense sticks, a ritual dagger, tarot cards, two red candles, occult themed pieces of jewelry, several pieces of wood from the local craft store, a wood burning tool, a porcelain doll, a plastic mask, a few empty bottles, and an old monocle from a grandparent. Of course there are many sorts of items that one might find use for in a toolbox. Perhaps instead of keeping an actual container, the magus simply keeps a stash of useable materials in the home, car, and office. There could be sigil paintings, blank books, and old pieces of circuit boards at home, while in the car there is a magical wand on the dashboard and an altar cloth draped over the back seat, and in the office their may be a few enchanted suit ties, a collection of occult spellcasting software, and the statue of an ancient god sitting on the desk. Just about anything that can be of personal magical significance, possess a powerful magical association, or be usefully symbolic is a viable element.

    The idea is that by keeping a full toolbox the magus will have access to materials that will aid in the creation of effective magical manifestations without having to go hunting about for useful components. Often the practitioner will not require physical items or accouterments to aid in the use of magick, though having such materials on hand is advantageous. Which leads to a more compact version of the toolbox, the sorcerer's kit. The kit is nothing more than a portable toolbox that can be carried on a personal level by the individual practitioner. For example, a magus that carries a backpack already may choose to include a cigarette lighter, a few vials of salt, a handwritten spellbook, blank sheets of paper, a portable music device, a compass, and a box of crayons. This way the magus will always have a multitude of items at his or her disposal with which to work more effective magick than had the items not been present. The author usually carries two pocket knives, sidewalk chalk, a handful of crystals, several feet of waxed string, matches, and a few blank pages of parchment. The key to kit creation is to make an effort to gauge what sorts of items you might find yourself in need of, meaning that one magi's kit will be quite different from another's.

Expanding Worldview

As has been shown, tactical magick is a system based on associations, symbology, and personal relevance. Though even as it exists as a magical system it can be used as a style with which one uses other systems. It is a versatile magical practice that can be adapted to any practitioner or magical system according to personal, socio-cultural, and magical needs. This path of magick feeds on knowledge and understanding of the hermetic relationships that make up reality.

It is important for the practitioner, regardless of situation or agendas, to continue both the magical and academic education. Study history and science, explore philosophy and religion, become familiar with art, culture, and music. The more that a practitioner knows, especially in the areas of culture, science, and the occult, the more vast the practitioner's resources for magical significance will be. For example, knowing the history and culture behind the various systems of magical symbols, ancient runes, and writing systems, the more capable the practitioner will be of drawing upon those elements of reality in such a manner as to be useful in any situation. The more a practitioner knows and understands the natural world through the study of physics and chemistry the more able he or she will be at manifesting the will within the physical and etheric realms. Imagine how greatly the discipline of physics has influenced the study of magick, or how much of an impact modern chemistry has had on alchemy. By staying informed and ideally having at least a functional knowledge of these subjects, the better able the practitioner will be at taking advantage of the advancements of science, culture, and art in relation to the practice of magick. The more you know about science, culture, and art the more of a 'database' of associations, symbols, relationships, and magically significant elements of reality you will have at your fingertips.

Survival is evolution, and necessity is the catalyst of innovation.

Printed in the United Kingdom
by Lightning Source UK Ltd.
129252UK00002B/365/A